HARD NUTS OF HISTORY

Play the Game

D0733751

TRACEY TURNER

ILLUSTRATED BY JAMIE LENMAN

A & C BLACK
AN IMPRINT OF BLOOMSBURY
LONDON NEW DELHI NEW YORK SYDNEY

First published 2015 by

A & C Black, an imprint of Bloomsbury Publishing Plc

50 Bedford Square, London WC1B 3DP

www.bloomsbury.com

Bloomsbury is a registered trademark of Bloomsbury Publishing Plc

Copyright © 2015 A & C Black

Text copyright © 2015 Tracey Turner

Illustrations copyright © 2015 Jamie Lenman
Additional images © Shutterstock

The rights of Tracey Turner and Jamie Lenman to be identified as the author and illustrator of this work respectively, has been asserted by them in accordance with the Copyrights, Designs and Patents Act 1988.

ISBN 978-1-4729-1097-4

A CIP catalogue for this book is available from the British Library.

All rights reserved. No part of this publication may be reproduced in any form or by any means – graphic, electronic or mechanical, including photocopying, recording, taping or information storage and retrieval systems – without the prior permission in writing of the publishers.

This book is produced using paper that is made from wood grown in managed, sustainable forests. It is natural, renewable and recyclable. The logging and manufacturing processes conform to the environmental regulations of the country of origin.

Printed in China by Leo Paper Products, Heshan, Guangdong

1 3 5 7 9 10 8 6 4 2

INTRODUCTION

Prepare to do battle with some of the hardest nuts of history . . .

FIND OUT . . .

- **Who was the bravest ancient Greek warrior?**
- **Which was the most ruthless Roman general?**
- **Who was the most cunning warrior of all?**
- **Which intrepid explorer had the best survival skills?**
- **Who was the hardest nut of myths and legends?**

Some of these hard nuts won battles, some conquered empires, and some started revolutions. They ruled millions of subjects, crossed uncharted territory, killed terrifying monsters and all of them were as hard as nails. Each tough nut character has a rating for cunning, courage, survival skills and ruthlessness. They are also surrounded by a different colour to indicate where they come from or what they did:

Blue: Ancient Greece	Purple: Wars and Battles
Yellow: Ancient Rome	Dark Green: Travellers and Explorers
Green: Ancient Egypt	Dark Red: Kings and Queens
Red: Warriors	Turquoise: Myths and Legends

Play the game and take on your friends and family to find out if Cleopatra was more cunning than Julius Caesar, or whether Wellington had better survival skills than Napoleon.

Turn the page for instructions on how to play.

BATTLE OF THE HARD NUTS

HOW TO PLAY

This game can be played by two or more players. Cut out the cards and shuffle and deal an equal number to each player. The player who starts must choose a category from his or her topmost card. They can choose from either the *Hardometer* scores or the overall *Hard Nut Rating*.

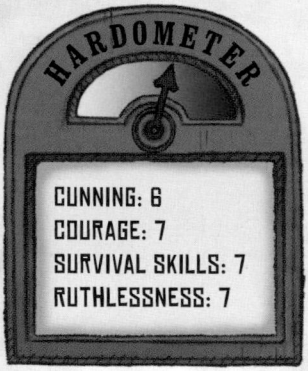

The other players must then give the score for the same category from their top card. The player with the highest score wins the opposing player's top card/s. In the event of a draw, the cards are placed in the centre and a new category is selected from the next card by the same person.

The winner of that round gets all of the cards in the centre as well as the top card from each player.

The winner is the player who obtains the whole pack. Good luck, and may the hardest nut win!

BUCEPHALIA
ALEXANDRIA
ALEXANDRIA
ALEXANDRIA
ALEXANDRIA
ALEXANDRIA
ALEXANDRIA
ALEXANDRIA
ALEXANDRIA
ALEXANDRIA
ALEXANDRIA
ALEXANDRIA
ALEXANDRIA
ALEXANDRIA
HARDOMETER
CUNNING: 8
COURAGE: 8
SURVIVAL SKILLS: 8
RUTHLESSNESS: 9
HARD NUT RATING: 8.3
ALEXANDER THE GREAT

JULIUS CAESAR
HARD NUT RATING: 8.3
HARDOMETER
CUNNING: 8
COURAGE: 9
SURVIVAL SKILLS: 7
RUTHLESSNESS: 9

CLEOPATRA
HARD NUT RATING: 7.8
HARDOMETER
CUNNING: 8
COURAGE: 8
SURVIVAL SKILLS: 7
RUTHLESSNESS: 8

BABUR
HARD NUT RATING: 8.5
HARDOMETER
CUNNING: 9
COURAGE: 8
SURVIVAL SKILLS: 9
RUTHLESSNESS: 8

HARD NUTS OF HISTORY

A & C BLACK
AN IMPRINT OF BLOOMSBURY
LONDON NEW DELHI NEW YORK SYDNEY

HARD NUTS OF HISTORY

A & C BLACK
AN IMPRINT OF BLOOMSBURY
LONDON NEW DELHI NEW YORK SYDNEY

HARD NUTS OF HISTORY

A & C BLACK
AN IMPRINT OF BLOOMSBURY
LONDON NEW DELHI NEW YORK SYDNEY

HARD NUTS OF HISTORY

A & C BLACK
AN IMPRINT OF BLOOMSBURY
LONDON NEW DELHI NEW YORK SYDNEY

HARD NUT RATING: 6.8
HARDOMETER
CUNNING: 6
COURAGE: 7
SURVIVAL SKILLS: 7
RUTHLESSNESS: 7
CHRISTOPHER COLUMBUS

HERACLES
HARD NUT RATING: 10
HARDOMETER
CUNNING: 10
COURAGE: 10
SURVIVAL SKILLS: 10
RUTHLESSNESS: 10

FERDINAND AND ISABELLA
HARDOMETER
CUNNING: 7
COURAGE: 6
SURVIVAL SKILLS: 9
RUTHLESSNESS: 9
HARD NUT RATING: 7.8

THE DUKE OF WELLINGTON
HARD NUT RATING: 8.3
HARDOMETER
CUNNING: 9
COURAGE: 8
SURVIVAL SKILLS: 8
RUTHLESSNESS: 8

HARD NUTS OF HISTORY

A & C BLACK
AN IMPRINT OF BLOOMSBURY
LONDON NEW DELHI NEW YORK SYDNEY

HARD NUTS OF HISTORY

A & C BLACK
AN IMPRINT OF BLOOMSBURY
LONDON NEW DELHI NEW YORK SYDNEY

HARD NUTS OF HISTORY

A & C BLACK
AN IMPRINT OF BLOOMSBURY
LONDON NEW DELHI NEW YORK SYDNEY

HARD NUTS OF HISTORY

A & C BLACK
AN IMPRINT OF BLOOMSBURY
LONDON NEW DELHI NEW YORK SYDNEY

SIMÓN BOLÍVAR
HARD NUT RATING: 7.3
HARDOMETER
CUNNING: 7
COURAGE: 8
SURVIVAL SKILLS: 6
RUTHLESSNESS: 8
HARALD HARDRADA
HARD NUT RATING: 7
HARDOMETER
CUNNING: 6
COURAGE: 9
SURVIVAL SKILLS: 5
RUTHLESSNESS: 8
AUGUSTUS CAESAR
FIRST CITIZEN
HARD NUT RATING: 9
HARDOMETER
CUNNING: 9
COURAGE: 9
SURVIVAL SKILLS: 9
RUTHLESSNESS: 9
HARDOMETER
CUNNING: 7
COURAGE: 10
SURVIVAL SKILLS: 6
RUTHLESSNESS: 7
HARD NUT RATING: 7.5
LEONIDAS

HARD NUTS OF HISTORY

A & C BLACK
AN IMPRINT OF BLOOMSBURY
LONDON NEW DELHI NEW YORK SYDNEY

HARD NUTS OF HISTORY

A & C BLACK
AN IMPRINT OF BLOOMSBURY
LONDON NEW DELHI NEW YORK SYDNEY

HARD NUTS OF HISTORY

A & C BLACK
AN IMPRINT OF BLOOMSBURY
LONDON NEW DELHI NEW YORK SYDNEY

HARD NUTS OF HISTORY

A & C BLACK
AN IMPRINT OF BLOOMSBURY
LONDON NEW DELHI NEW YORK SYDNEY

HARD NUT RATING: 8.5
HARDOMETER
CUNNING: 8
COURAGE: 8
SURVIVAL SKILLS: 9
RUTHLESSNESS: 9
GENGHIS KHAN

KING PIYE
HARDOMETER
CUNNING: 9
COURAGE: 9
SURVIVAL SKILLS: 9
RUTHLESSNESS: 9
HARD NUT RATING: 9

BEOWULF
HARD NUT RATING: 9.8
HARDOMETER
CUNNING: 10
COURAGE: 10
SURVIVAL SKILLS: 9
RUTHLESSNESS: 10

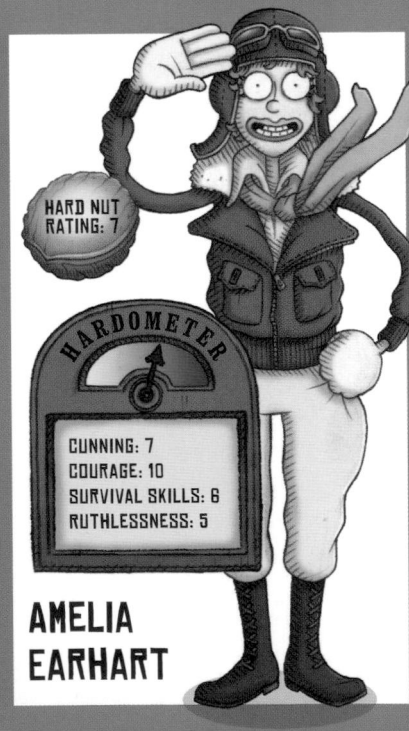
HARD NUT RATING: 7
HARDOMETER
CUNNING: 7
COURAGE: 10
SURVIVAL SKILLS: 6
RUTHLESSNESS: 5
AMELIA EARHART

HARD NUTS OF HISTORY

A & C BLACK
AN IMPRINT OF BLOOMSBURY
LONDON NEW DELHI NEW YORK SYDNEY

HARD NUTS OF HISTORY

A & C BLACK
AN IMPRINT OF BLOOMSBURY
LONDON NEW DELHI NEW YORK SYDNEY

HARD NUTS OF HISTORY

A & C BLACK
AN IMPRINT OF BLOOMSBURY
LONDON NEW DELHI NEW YORK SYDNEY

HARD NUTS OF HISTORY

A & C BLACK
AN IMPRINT OF BLOOMSBURY
LONDON NEW DELHI NEW YORK SYDNEY

HARD NUT RATING: 5
HARDOMETER
CUNNING: 5
COURAGE: 10
SURVIVAL SKILLS: 5
RUTHLESSNESS: 0
SOCRATES

HANNIBAL
HARD NUT RATING: 7.8
HARDOMETER
CUNNING: 8
COURAGE: 9
SURVIVAL SKILLS: 8
RUTHLESSNESS: 6

TUTANKHAMUN
HARD NUT RATING: 6.3
HARDOMETER
CUNNING: 6
COURAGE: 8
SURVIVAL SKILLS: 4
RUTHLESSNESS: 7

GERONIMO
HARD NUT RATING: 8.3
HARDOMETER
CUNNING: 7
COURAGE: 9
SURVIVAL SKILLS: 8
RUTHLESSNESS: 9

HARD NUTS OF HISTORY

A & C BLACK
AN IMPRINT OF BLOOMSBURY
LONDON NEW DELHI NEW YORK SYDNEY

HARD NUTS OF HISTORY

A & C BLACK
AN IMPRINT OF BLOOMSBURY
LONDON NEW DELHI NEW YORK SYDNEY

HARD NUTS OF HISTORY

A & C BLACK
AN IMPRINT OF BLOOMSBURY
LONDON NEW DELHI NEW YORK SYDNEY

HARD NUTS OF HISTORY

A & C BLACK
AN IMPRINT OF BLOOMSBURY
LONDON NEW DELHI NEW YORK SYDNEY

HARD NUT RATING: 8.3
HARDOMETER
CUNNING: 8
COURAGE: 9
SURVIVAL SKILLS: 8
RUTHLESSNESS: 8
CAPTAIN COOK
HUA MULAN
HARD NUT RATING: 9
HARDOMETER
CUNNING: 10
COURAGE: 9
SURVIVAL SKILLS: 9
RUTHLESSNESS: 8
NZINGA MBANDE
HARD NUT RATING: 7.5
HARDOMETER
CUNNING: 8
COURAGE: 8
SURVIVAL SKILLS: 9
RUTHLESSNESS: 5
LEON TROTSKY
HARD NUT RATING: 8
HARDOMETER
CUNNING: 9
COURAGE: 9
SURVIVAL SKILLS: 7
RUTHLESSNESS: 7

HARD NUTS OF HISTORY

A & C BLACK
AN IMPRINT OF BLOOMSBURY
LONDON NEW DELHI NEW YORK SYDNEY

HARD NUTS OF HISTORY

A & C BLACK
AN IMPRINT OF BLOOMSBURY
LONDON NEW DELHI NEW YORK SYDNEY

HARD NUTS OF HISTORY

A & C BLACK
AN IMPRINT OF BLOOMSBURY
LONDON NEW DELHI NEW YORK SYDNEY

HARD NUTS OF HISTORY

A & C BLACK
AN IMPRINT OF BLOOMSBURY
LONDON NEW DELHI NEW YORK SYDNEY

GENERAL CUSTER
HARD NUT RATING: 8.3
HARDOMETER
CUNNING: 7
COURAGE: 9
SURVIVAL SKILLS: 8
RUTHLESSNESS: 9
HENRY VIII
HARD NUT RATING: 7.3
HARDOMETER
CUNNING: 8
COURAGE: 6
SURVIVAL SKILLS: 5
RUTHLESSNESS: 10
SPARTACUS
HARDOMETER
CUNNING: 9
COURAGE: 9
SURVIVAL SKILLS: 7
RUTHLESSNESS: 7
HARD NUT RATING: 8
HYPATIA
HARDOMETER
HARD NUT RATING: 6.3
CUNNING: 5
COURAGE: 9
SURVIVAL SKILLS: 6
RUTHLESSNESS: 5

HARD NUTS OF HISTORY

A & C BLACK
AN IMPRINT OF BLOOMSBURY
LONDON NEW DELHI NEW YORK SYDNEY

HARD NUTS OF HISTORY

A & C BLACK
AN IMPRINT OF BLOOMSBURY
LONDON NEW DELHI NEW YORK SYDNEY

HARD NUTS OF HISTORY

A & C BLACK
AN IMPRINT OF BLOOMSBURY
LONDON NEW DELHI NEW YORK SYDNEY

HARD NUTS OF HISTORY

A & C BLACK
AN IMPRINT OF BLOOMSBURY
LONDON NEW DELHI NEW YORK SYDNEY

JOAN OF ARC
HARD NUT RATING: 7
HARDOMETER
CUNNING: 7
COURAGE: 9
SURVIVAL SKILLS: 5
RUTHLESSNESS: 7

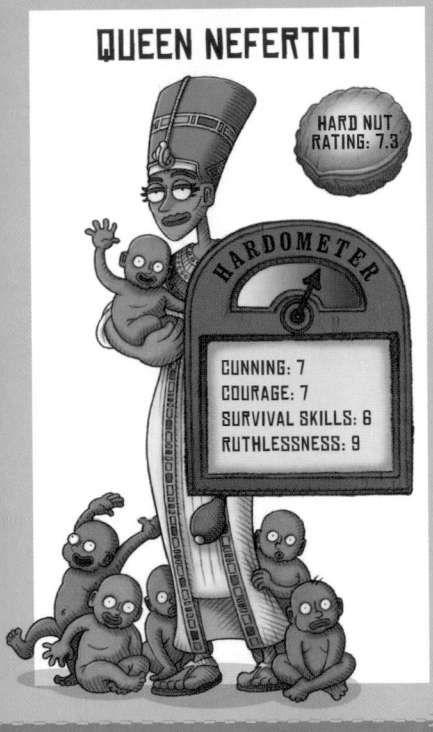
QUEEN NEFERTITI
HARD NUT RATING: 7.3
HARDOMETER
CUNNING: 7
COURAGE: 7
SURVIVAL SKILLS: 6
RUTHLESSNESS: 9

CÚ CHULAINN
HARD NUT RATING: 8.3
HARDOMETER
CUNNING: 8
COURAGE: 9
SURVIVAL SKILLS: 7
RUTHLESSNESS: 9

HERNÁN CORTÉS
HARD NUT RATING: 8.8
HARDOMETER
CUNNING: 8
COURAGE: 9
SURVIVAL SKILLS: 8
RUTHLESSNESS: 10

HARD NUTS OF HISTORY

A & C BLACK
AN IMPRINT OF BLOOMSBURY
LONDON NEW DELHI NEW YORK SYDNEY

HARD NUTS OF HISTORY

A & C BLACK
AN IMPRINT OF BLOOMSBURY
LONDON NEW DELHI NEW YORK SYDNEY

HARD NUTS OF HISTORY

A & C BLACK
AN IMPRINT OF BLOOMSBURY
LONDON NEW DELHI NEW YORK SYDNEY

HARD NUTS OF HISTORY

A & C BLACK
AN IMPRINT OF BLOOMSBURY
LONDON NEW DELHI NEW YORK SYDNEY

ARCHIMEDES
HARD NUT RATING: 6.3
EUREKA!
HARDOMETER
CUNNING: 8
COURAGE: 8
SURVIVAL SKILLS: 5
RUTHLESSNESS: 4

EMPEROR NERO
HARD NUT RATING: 7.8
HARDOMETER
CUNNING: 7
COURAGE: 8
SURVIVAL SKILLS: 6
RUTHLESSNESS: 10

THUTMOSE III
HARD NUT RATING: 9
HARDOMETER
CUNNING: 9
COURAGE: 9
SURVIVAL SKILLS: 9
RUTHLESSNESS: 9

TOMYRIS
HARD NUT RATING: 9.3
HARDOMETER
CUNNING: 9
COURAGE: 9
SURVIVAL SKILLS: 10
RUTHLESSNESS: 9

HARD NUTS OF HISTORY

A & C BLACK
AN IMPRINT OF BLOOMSBURY
LONDON NEW DELHI NEW YORK SYDNEY

HARD NUTS OF HISTORY

A & C BLACK
AN IMPRINT OF BLOOMSBURY
LONDON NEW DELHI NEW YORK SYDNEY

HARD NUTS OF HISTORY

A & C BLACK
AN IMPRINT OF BLOOMSBURY
LONDON NEW DELHI NEW YORK SYDNEY

HARD NUTS OF HISTORY

A & C BLACK
AN IMPRINT OF BLOOMSBURY
LONDON NEW DELHI NEW YORK SYDNEY

VINLAND
HARD NUT RATING: 8.5
HARDOMETER
CUNNING: 8
COURAGE: 9
SURVIVAL SKILLS: 9
RUTHLESSNESS: 8
LEIF ERICSON

THOR
HARD NUT RATING: 9.3
HARDOMETER
CUNNING: 8
COURAGE: 10
SURVIVAL SKILLS: 9
RUTHLESSNESS: 10

KING KAMEHAMEHA I
HARD NUT RATING: 8
HARDOMETER
CUNNING: 8
COURAGE: 9
SURVIVAL SKILLS: 7
RUTHLESSNESS: 8

FLORA SANDES
HARD NUT RATING: 8
HARDOMETER
CUNNING: 8
COURAGE: 10
SURVIVAL SKILLS: 8
RUTHLESSNESS: 6

HARD NUTS OF HISTORY

A & C BLACK
AN IMPRINT OF BLOOMSBURY
LONDON NEW DELHI NEW YORK SYDNEY

HARD NUTS OF HISTORY

A & C BLACK
AN IMPRINT OF BLOOMSBURY
LONDON NEW DELHI NEW YORK SYDNEY

HARD NUTS OF HISTORY

A & C BLACK
AN IMPRINT OF BLOOMSBURY
LONDON NEW DELHI NEW YORK SYDNEY

HARD NUTS OF HISTORY

A & C BLACK
AN IMPRINT OF BLOOMSBURY
LONDON NEW DELHI NEW YORK SYDNEY

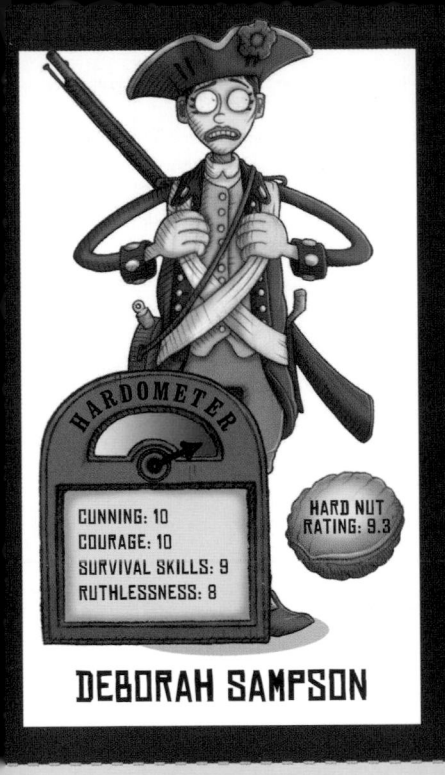
HARDOMETER
CUNNING: 10
COURAGE: 10
SURVIVAL SKILLS: 9
RUTHLESSNESS: 8
HARD NUT RATING: 9.3
DEBORAH SAMPSON

KING SHAKA
HARD NUT RATING: 8
HARDOMETER
CUNNING: 8
COURAGE: 7
SURVIVAL SKILLS: 7
RUTHLESSNESS: 10

AGRIPPINA
HARD NUT RATING: 8.8
HARDOMETER
CUNNING: 9
COURAGE: 9
SURVIVAL SKILLS: 8
RUTHLESSNESS: 9

DARIUS THE GREAT
HARD NUT RATING: 8.5
HARDOMETER
CUNNING: 9
COURAGE: 8
SURVIVAL SKILLS: 8
RUTHLESSNESS: 9

HARD NUTS OF HISTORY

A & C BLACK
AN IMPRINT OF BLOOMSBURY
LONDON NEW DELHI NEW YORK SYDNEY

HARD NUTS OF HISTORY

A & C BLACK
AN IMPRINT OF BLOOMSBURY
LONDON NEW DELHI NEW YORK SYDNEY

HARD NUTS OF HISTORY

A & C BLACK
AN IMPRINT OF BLOOMSBURY
LONDON NEW DELHI NEW YORK SYDNEY

HARD NUTS OF HISTORY

A & C BLACK
AN IMPRINT OF BLOOMSBURY
LONDON NEW DELHI NEW YORK SYDNEY

CHARLEMAGNE
HARD NUT RATING: 8
HARDOMETER
CUNNING: 8
COURAGE: 8
SURVIVAL SKILLS: 8
RUTHLESSNESS: 8

SNEFRU
HARD NUT RATING: 7.5
HARDOMETER
CUNNING: 7
COURAGE: 8
SURVIVAL SKILLS: 8
RUTHLESSNESS: 7

DURGA
HARD NUT RATING: 9
HARDOMETER
CUNNING: 9
COURAGE: 9
SURVIVAL SKILLS: 9
RUTHLESSNESS: 9

FERDINAND MAGELLAN
HARD NUT RATING: 8.3
HARDOMETER
CUNNING: 8
COURAGE: 9
SURVIVAL SKILLS: 6
RUTHLESSNESS: 10

HARD NUTS OF HISTORY

A & C BLACK
AN IMPRINT OF BLOOMSBURY
LONDON NEW DELHI NEW YORK SYDNEY

HARD NUTS OF HISTORY

A & C BLACK
AN IMPRINT OF BLOOMSBURY
LONDON NEW DELHI NEW YORK SYDNEY

HARD NUTS OF HISTORY

A & C BLACK
AN IMPRINT OF BLOOMSBURY
LONDON NEW DELHI NEW YORK SYDNEY

HARD NUTS OF HISTORY

A & C BLACK
AN IMPRINT OF BLOOMSBURY
LONDON NEW DELHI NEW YORK SYDNEY

PHEIDIPPIDES
HARDOMETER
CUNNING: 6
COURAGE: 9
SURVIVAL SKILLS: 6
RUTHLESSNESS: 5
HARD NUT RATING: 6.5

HARD NUT RATING: 8
HARDOMETER
CUNNING: 8
COURAGE: 9
SURVIVAL SKILLS: 7
RUTHLESSNESS: 8
MARK ANTONY

HATSHEPSUT
HARD NUT RATING: 8.8
HARDOMETER
CUNNING: 10
COURAGE: 8
SURVIVAL SKILLS: 9
RUTHLESSNESS: 8

TOMOE GOZEN
HARDOMETER
CUNNING: 7
COURAGE: 9
SURVIVAL SKILLS: 6
RUTHLESSNESS: 8
HARD NUT RATING: 7.5

HARD NUTS OF HISTORY

A & C BLACK
AN IMPRINT OF BLOOMSBURY
LONDON NEW DELHI NEW YORK SYDNEY

HARD NUTS OF HISTORY

A & C BLACK
AN IMPRINT OF BLOOMSBURY
LONDON NEW DELHI NEW YORK SYDNEY

HARD NUTS OF HISTORY

A & C BLACK
AN IMPRINT OF BLOOMSBURY
LONDON NEW DELHI NEW YORK SYDNEY

HARD NUTS OF HISTORY

A & C BLACK
AN IMPRINT OF BLOOMSBURY
LONDON NEW DELHI NEW YORK SYDNEY

MARCO POLO
HARDOMETER
CUNNING: 8
COURAGE: 8
SURVIVAL SKILLS: 8
RUTHLESSNESS: 7
HARD NUT RATING: 7.8

MEDEA
HARD NUT RATING: 9.5
HARDOMETER
CUNNING: 10
COURAGE: 8
SURVIVAL SKILLS: 10
RUTHLESSNESS: 10

FREDERICK THE GREAT
HARD NUT RATING: 7.5
HARDOMETER
CUNNING: 7
COURAGE: 7
SURVIVAL SKILLS: 8
RUTHLESSNESS: 8

DAVY CROCKETT
HARD NUT RATING: 7.3
HARDOMETER
CUNNING: 7
COURAGE: 9
SURVIVAL SKILLS: 5
RUTHLESSNESS: 8

HARD NUTS OF HISTORY

A & C BLACK
AN IMPRINT OF BLOOMSBURY
LONDON NEW DELHI NEW YORK SYDNEY

HARD NUTS OF HISTORY

A & C BLACK
AN IMPRINT OF BLOOMSBURY
LONDON NEW DELHI NEW YORK SYDNEY

HARD NUTS OF HISTORY

A & C BLACK
AN IMPRINT OF BLOOMSBURY
LONDON NEW DELHI NEW YORK SYDNEY

HARD NUTS OF HISTORY

A & C BLACK
AN IMPRINT OF BLOOMSBURY
LONDON NEW DELHI NEW YORK SYDNEY

MARY SEACOLE
HARD NUT RATING: 8.3
HARDOMETER
CUNNING: 9
COURAGE: 10
SURVIVAL SKILLS: 9
RUTHLESSNESS: 5
MONTEZUMA II
HARD NUT RATING: 7.5
HARDOMETER
CUNNING: 7
COURAGE: 8
SURVIVAL SKILLS: 6
RUTHLESSNESS: 9
POMPEY THE GREAT
HARD NUT RATING: 8.8
HARDOMETER
CUNNING: 9
COURAGE: 9
SURVIVAL SKILLS: 8
RUTHLESSNESS: 9
XERXES THE GREAT
HARD NUT RATING: 7.5
HARDOMETER
CUNNING: 6
COURAGE: 7
SURVIVAL SKILLS: 7
RUTHLESSNESS: 10

HARD NUTS OF HISTORY

A & C BLACK
AN IMPRINT OF BLOOMSBURY
LONDON NEW DELHI NEW YORK SYDNEY

HARD NUTS OF HISTORY

A & C BLACK
AN IMPRINT OF BLOOMSBURY
LONDON NEW DELHI NEW YORK SYDNEY

HARD NUTS OF HISTORY

A & C BLACK
AN IMPRINT OF BLOOMSBURY
LONDON NEW DELHI NEW YORK SYDNEY

HARD NUTS OF HISTORY

A & C BLACK
AN IMPRINT OF BLOOMSBURY
LONDON NEW DELHI NEW YORK SYDNEY

TIMUR
HARD NUT RATING: 9.3
HARDOMETER
CUNNING: 9
COURAGE: 9
SURVIVAL SKILLS: 9
RUTHLESSNESS: 10
KING NARMER
HARD NUT RATING: 8.8
HARDOMETER
CUNNING: 9
COURAGE: 9
SURVIVAL SKILLS: 8
RUTHLESSNESS: 9
THUGINE
HARD NUT RATING: 8.3
HARDOMETER
CUNNING: 8
COURAGE: 8
SURVIVAL SKILLS: 9
RUTHLESSNESS: 8
NEIL ARMSTRONG
HARD NUT RATING: 8.5
NASA
HARDOMETER
CUNNING: 8
COURAGE: 10
SURVIVAL SKILLS: 9
RUTHLESSNESS: 7

HARD NUTS OF HISTORY

A & C BLACK
AN IMPRINT OF BLOOMSBURY
LONDON NEW DELHI NEW YORK SYDNEY

HARD NUTS OF HISTORY

A & C BLACK
AN IMPRINT OF BLOOMSBURY
LONDON NEW DELHI NEW YORK SYDNEY

HARD NUTS OF HISTORY

A & C BLACK
AN IMPRINT OF BLOOMSBURY
LONDON NEW DELHI NEW YORK SYDNEY

HARD NUTS OF HISTORY

A & C BLACK
AN IMPRINT OF BLOOMSBURY
LONDON NEW DELHI NEW YORK SYDNEY

HARD NUT RATING: 9
HARDOMETER
CUNNING: 9
COURAGE: 10
SURVIVAL SKILLS: 8
RUTHLESSNESS: 9
PELOPIDAS

ZENOBIA
HARD NUT RATING: 8.8
HARDOMETER
CUNNING: 9
COURAGE: 9
SURVIVAL SKILLS: 9
RUTHLESSNESS: 8

HARD NUT RATING: 9
HARDOMETER
CUNNING: 9
COURAGE: 9
SURVIVAL SKILLS: 10
RUTHLESSNESS: 8
RAMESSES THE GREAT

ATTILA THE HUN
HARDOMETER
CUNNING: 9
COURAGE: 8
SURVIVAL SKILLS: 9
RUTHLESSNESS: 10
HARD NUT RATING: 9

HARD NUTS OF HISTORY

A & C BLACK
AN IMPRINT OF BLOOMSBURY
LONDON NEW DELHI NEW YORK SYDNEY

HARD NUTS OF HISTORY

A & C BLACK
AN IMPRINT OF BLOOMSBURY
LONDON NEW DELHI NEW YORK SYDNEY

HARD NUTS OF HISTORY

A & C BLACK
AN IMPRINT OF BLOOMSBURY
LONDON NEW DELHI NEW YORK SYDNEY

HARD NUTS OF HISTORY

A & C BLACK
AN IMPRINT OF BLOOMSBURY
LONDON NEW DELHI NEW YORK SYDNEY

MARY KINGSLEY
HARDOMETER
CUNNING: 5
COURAGE: 9
SURVIVAL SKILLS: 8
RUTHLESSNESS: 5
HARD NUT RATING: 6.8

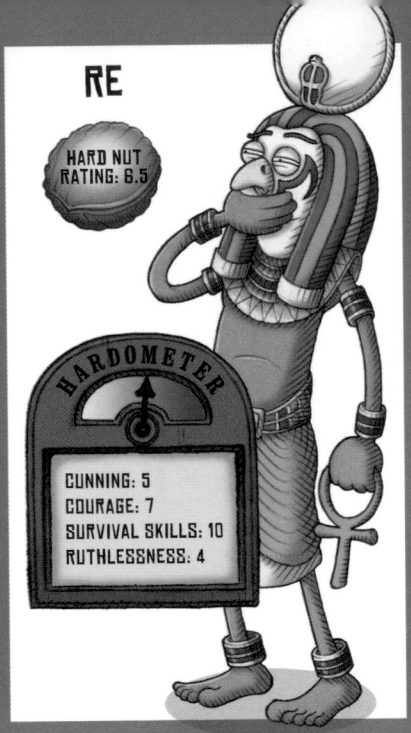
RE
HARD NUT RATING: 6.5
HARDOMETER
CUNNING: 5
COURAGE: 7
SURVIVAL SKILLS: 10
RUTHLESSNESS: 4

MURAD IV
HARD NUT RATING: 7.8
HARDOMETER
CUNNING: 8
COURAGE: 8
SURVIVAL SKILLS: 6
RUTHLESSNESS: 9

HARD NUT RATING: 8
HARDOMETER
CUNNING: 8
COURAGE: 8
SURVIVAL SKILLS: 8
RUTHLESSNESS: 8
ROBERT E LEE

HARD NUTS OF HISTORY

A & C BLACK
AN IMPRINT OF BLOOMSBURY
LONDON NEW DELHI NEW YORK SYDNEY

HARD NUTS OF HISTORY

A & C BLACK
AN IMPRINT OF BLOOMSBURY
LONDON NEW DELHI NEW YORK SYDNEY

HARD NUTS OF HISTORY

A & C BLACK
AN IMPRINT OF BLOOMSBURY
LONDON NEW DELHI NEW YORK SYDNEY

HARD NUTS OF HISTORY

A & C BLACK
AN IMPRINT OF BLOOMSBURY
LONDON NEW DELHI NEW YORK SYDNEY

CHE GUEVARA
HARD NUT RATING: 7.8
HARDOMETER
CUNNING: 7
COURAGE: 7
SURVIVAL SKILLS: 8
RUTHLESSNESS: 9
HARD NUT RATING: 7.3
HARDOMETER
CUNNING: 7
COURAGE: 7
SURVIVAL SKILLS: 8
RUTHLESSNESS: 7
ELIZABETH I
EMPEROR HADRIAN
HARD NUT RATING: 8.5
HARDOMETER
CUNNING: 8
COURAGE: 8
SURVIVAL SKILLS: 9
RUTHLESSNESS: 9
HIPPOCRATES
HARD NUT RATING: 6.3
HARDOMETER
CUNNING: 4
COURAGE: 9
SURVIVAL SKILLS: 8
RUTHLESSNESS: 4

HARD NUTS OF HISTORY

A & C BLACK
AN IMPRINT OF BLOOMSBURY
LONDON NEW DELHI NEW YORK SYDNEY

HARD NUTS OF HISTORY

A & C BLACK
AN IMPRINT OF BLOOMSBURY
LONDON NEW DELHI NEW YORK SYDNEY

HARD NUTS OF HISTORY

A & C BLACK
AN IMPRINT OF BLOOMSBURY
LONDON NEW DELHI NEW YORK SYDNEY

HARD NUTS OF HISTORY

A & C BLACK
AN IMPRINT OF BLOOMSBURY
LONDON NEW DELHI NEW YORK SYDNEY

THE TRUNG SISTERS
HARD NUT RATING: 7.8
HARDOMETER
CUNNING: 8
COURAGE: 9
SURVIVAL SKILLS: 6
RUTHLESSNESS: 8

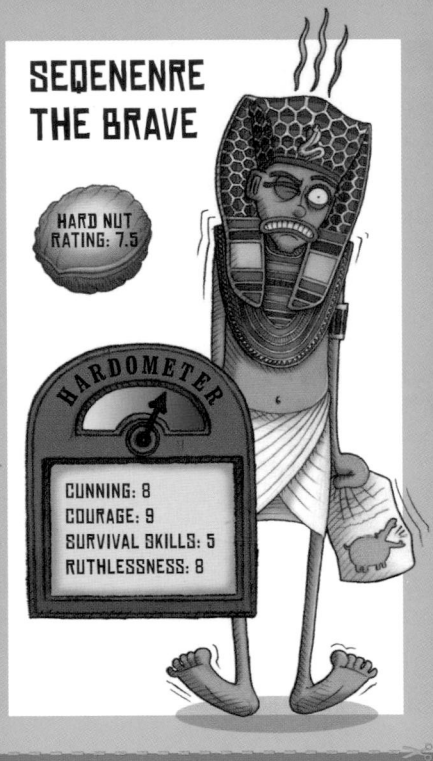
SEQENENRE THE BRAVE
HARD NUT RATING: 7.5
HARDOMETER
CUNNING: 8
COURAGE: 9
SURVIVAL SKILLS: 5
RUTHLESSNESS: 8

ROBIN HOOD
HARD NUT RATING: 8
HARDOMETER
CUNNING: 8
COURAGE: 9
SURVIVAL SKILLS: 8
RUTHLESSNESS: 7

SCOTT OF THE ANTARCTIC
HARD NUT RATING: 7
HARDOMETER
CUNNING: 5
COURAGE: 9
SURVIVAL SKILLS: 8
RUTHLESSNESS: 6

HARD NUTS OF HISTORY

A & C BLACK
AN IMPRINT OF BLOOMSBURY
LONDON NEW DELHI NEW YORK SYDNEY

HARD NUTS OF HISTORY

A & C BLACK
AN IMPRINT OF BLOOMSBURY
LONDON NEW DELHI NEW YORK SYDNEY

HARD NUTS OF HISTORY

A & C BLACK
AN IMPRINT OF BLOOMSBURY
LONDON NEW DELHI NEW YORK SYDNEY

HARD NUTS OF HISTORY

A & C BLACK
AN IMPRINT OF BLOOMSBURY
LONDON NEW DELHI NEW YORK SYDNEY

PISISTRATUS
HARD NUT RATING: 8.5
HARDOMETER
CUNNING: 9
COURAGE: 8
SURVIVAL SKILLS: 9
RUTHLESSNESS: 8

SULLA
HARD NUT RATING: 10
PROSCRIPTIONS
HARDOMETER
CUNNING: 10
COURAGE: 10
SURVIVAL SKILLS: 10
RUTHLESSNESS: 10

HARD NUT RATING: 8.8
HARDOMETER
CUNNING: 9
COURAGE: 9
SURVIVAL SKILLS: 9
RUTHLESSNESS: 8
PTOLEMY I

MAHMUD OF GHAZNI
HARD NUT RATING: 8
HARDOMETER
CUNNING: 7
COURAGE: 8
SURVIVAL SKILLS: 8
RUTHLESSNESS: 9

HARD NUTS OF HISTORY

A & C BLACK
AN IMPRINT OF BLOOMSBURY
LONDON NEW DELHI NEW YORK SYDNEY

HARD NUTS OF HISTORY

A & C BLACK
AN IMPRINT OF BLOOMSBURY
LONDON NEW DELHI NEW YORK SYDNEY

HARD NUTS OF HISTORY

A & C BLACK
AN IMPRINT OF BLOOMSBURY
LONDON NEW DELHI NEW YORK SYDNEY

HARD NUTS OF HISTORY

A & C BLACK
AN IMPRINT OF BLOOMSBURY
LONDON NEW DELHI NEW YORK SYDNEY

SIR WALTER RALEIGH
HARD NUT RATING: 7
HARDOMETER
CUNNING: 6
COURAGE: 8
SURVIVAL SKILLS: 7
RUTHLESSNESS: 7
THESEUS
HARD NUT RATING: 8
HARDOMETER
CUNNING: 7
COURAGE: 10
SURVIVAL SKILLS: 6
RUTHLESSNESS: 9
SULEIMAN THE MAGNIFICENT
HARD NUT RATING: 7
HARDOMETER
CUNNING: 7
COURAGE: 7
SURVIVAL SKILLS: 8
RUTHLESSNESS: 6
HARD NUT RATING: 9
HARDOMETER
CUNNING: 9
COURAGE: 10
SURVIVAL SKILLS: 8
RUTHLESSNESS: 9
VIOLETTE SZABO

HARD NUTS OF HISTORY

A & C BLACK
AN IMPRINT OF BLOOMSBURY
LONDON NEW DELHI NEW YORK SYDNEY

HARD NUTS OF HISTORY

A & C BLACK
AN IMPRINT OF BLOOMSBURY
LONDON NEW DELHI NEW YORK SYDNEY

HARD NUTS OF HISTORY

A & C BLACK
AN IMPRINT OF BLOOMSBURY
LONDON NEW DELHI NEW YORK SYDNEY

HARD NUTS OF HISTORY

A & C BLACK
AN IMPRINT OF BLOOMSBURY
LONDON NEW DELHI NEW YORK SYDNEY

ASHOKA THE GREAT
HARD NUT RATING: 6.3
HARDOMETER
CUNNING: 7
COURAGE: 8
SURVIVAL SKILLS: 5
RUTHLESSNESS: 5
WU ZETIAN
HARD NUT RATING: 8.5
HARDOMETER
CUNNING: 8
COURAGE: 8
SURVIVAL SKILLS: 9
RUTHLESSNESS: 9
FLAVIUS BELISARIUS
HARD NUT RATING: 9
HARDOMETER
CUNNING: 9
COURAGE: 9
SURVIVAL SKILLS: 9
RUTHLESSNESS: 9
CLEON
HARD NUT RATING: 8
WANTED
HARDOMETER
CUNNING: 7
COURAGE: 9
SURVIVAL SKILLS: 6
RUTHLESSNESS: 10

HARD NUTS OF HISTORY

A & C BLACK
AN IMPRINT OF BLOOMSBURY
LONDON NEW DELHI NEW YORK SYDNEY

HARD NUTS OF HISTORY

A & C BLACK
AN IMPRINT OF BLOOMSBURY
LONDON NEW DELHI NEW YORK SYDNEY

HARD NUTS OF HISTORY

A & C BLACK
AN IMPRINT OF BLOOMSBURY
LONDON NEW DELHI NEW YORK SYDNEY

HARD NUTS OF HISTORY

A & C BLACK
AN IMPRINT OF BLOOMSBURY
LONDON NEW DELHI NEW YORK SYDNEY

HONGWU
HARD NUT RATING: 9
HARDOMETER
CUNNING: 9
COURAGE: 9
SURVIVAL SKILLS: 9
RUTHLESSNESS: 9

ESARHADDON
HARD NUT RATING: 8.5
HARDOMETER
CUNNING: 8
COURAGE: 9
SURVIVAL SKILLS: 8
RUTHLESSNESS: 9

SIR GAWAIN
HARD NUT RATING: 7.8
HARDOMETER
CUNNING: 7
COURAGE: 9
SURVIVAL SKILLS: 7
RUTHLESSNESS: 8

PONCE DE LEON
HARD NUT RATING: 9
HARDOMETER
CUNNING: 9
COURAGE: 9
SURVIVAL SKILLS: 8
RUTHLESSNESS: 10

HARD NUTS OF HISTORY

A & C BLACK
AN IMPRINT OF BLOOMSBURY
LONDON NEW DELHI NEW YORK SYDNEY

HARD NUTS OF HISTORY

A & C BLACK
AN IMPRINT OF BLOOMSBURY
LONDON NEW DELHI NEW YORK SYDNEY

HARD NUTS OF HISTORY

A & C BLACK
AN IMPRINT OF BLOOMSBURY
LONDON NEW DELHI NEW YORK SYDNEY

HARD NUTS OF HISTORY

A & C BLACK
AN IMPRINT OF BLOOMSBURY
LONDON NEW DELHI NEW YORK SYDNEY

LYSANDER
HARD NUT RATING: 8.5
NAVARCH
DEPUTY ADMIRAL
HARDOMETER
CUNNING: 9
COURAGE: 8
SURVIVAL SKILLS: 9
RUTHLESSNESS: 8

TARQUIN THE PROUD
HARD NUT RATING: 8.3
HARDOMETER
CUNNING: 8
COURAGE: 7
SURVIVAL SKILLS: 9
RUTHLESSNESS: 9

MENTUHOTEP II
HARD NUT RATING: 8.5
FIGHTING TO DO
HARDOMETER
CUNNING: 8
COURAGE: 9
SURVIVAL SKILLS: 8
RUTHLESSNESS: 9

NAPOLEON
HARD NUT RATING: 8
HARDOMETER
CUNNING: 8
COURAGE: 8
SURVIVAL SKILLS: 8
RUTHLESSNESS: 8

HARD NUTS OF HISTORY

A & C BLACK
AN IMPRINT OF BLOOMSBURY
LONDON NEW DELHI NEW YORK SYDNEY

HARD NUTS OF HISTORY

A & C BLACK
AN IMPRINT OF BLOOMSBURY
LONDON NEW DELHI NEW YORK SYDNEY

HARD NUTS OF HISTORY

A & C BLACK
AN IMPRINT OF BLOOMSBURY
LONDON NEW DELHI NEW YORK SYDNEY

HARD NUTS OF HISTORY

A & C BLACK
AN IMPRINT OF BLOOMSBURY
LONDON NEW DELHI NEW YORK SYDNEY

VASCO DA GAMA
HARD NUT RATING: 9
HARDOMETER
CUNNING: 9
COURAGE: 9
SURVIVAL SKILLS: 9
RUTHLESSNESS: 9
ANANSI
HARD NUT RATING: 7.5
HARDOMETER
CUNNING: 10
COURAGE: 5
SURVIVAL SKILLS: 5
RUTHLESSNESS: 10
QUEEN TAMAR OF GEORGIA
HARD NUT RATING: 7
HARDOMETER
CUNNING: 8
COURAGE: 8
SURVIVAL SKILLS: 6
RUTHLESSNESS: 6
KING HAROLD
HARD NUT RATING: 7.8
HARDOMETER
CUNNING: 7
COURAGE: 8
SURVIVAL SKILLS: 7
RUTHLESSNESS: 9

HARD NUTS OF HISTORY

A & C BLACK
AN IMPRINT OF BLOOMSBURY
LONDON NEW DELHI NEW YORK SYDNEY

HARD NUTS OF HISTORY

A & C BLACK
AN IMPRINT OF BLOOMSBURY
LONDON NEW DELHI NEW YORK SYDNEY

HARD NUTS OF HISTORY

A & C BLACK
AN IMPRINT OF BLOOMSBURY
LONDON NEW DELHI NEW YORK SYDNEY

HARD NUTS OF HISTORY

A & C BLACK
AN IMPRINT OF BLOOMSBURY
LONDON NEW DELHI NEW YORK SYDNEY

KING CETSHWAYO
HARD NUT RATING: 8.5
HARDOMETER
CUNNING: 9
COURAGE: 9
SURVIVAL SKILLS: 7
RUTHLESSNESS: 9
QUEEN ARTEMISIA OF HALICARNASSUS
HARD NUT RATING: 8.3
HARDOMETER
CUNNING: 8
COURAGE: 9
SURVIVAL SKILLS: 8
RUTHLESSNESS: 8
VERCINGETORIX
HARD NUT RATING: 7.5
HARDOMETER
CUNNING: 7
COURAGE: 8
SURVIVAL SKILLS: 7
RUTHLESSNESS: 8
THEMISTOCLES
HARD NUT RATING: 8.5
HARDOMETER
CUNNING: 9
COURAGE: 9
SURVIVAL SKILLS: 7
RUTHLESSNESS: 9

HARD NUTS OF HISTORY

A & C BLACK
AN IMPRINT OF BLOOMSBURY
LONDON NEW DELHI NEW YORK SYDNEY

HARD NUTS OF HISTORY

A & C BLACK
AN IMPRINT OF BLOOMSBURY
LONDON NEW DELHI NEW YORK SYDNEY

HARD NUTS OF HISTORY

A & C BLACK
AN IMPRINT OF BLOOMSBURY
LONDON NEW DELHI NEW YORK SYDNEY

HARD NUTS OF HISTORY

A & C BLACK
AN IMPRINT OF BLOOMSBURY
LONDON NEW DELHI NEW YORK SYDNEY

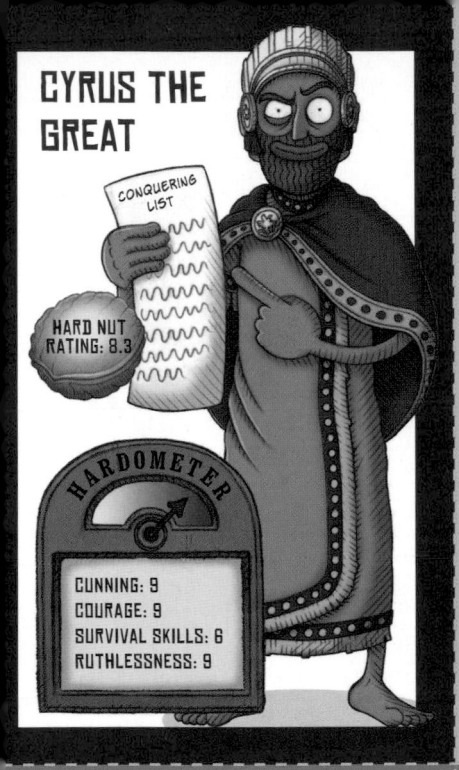
CYRUS THE GREAT
CONQUERING LIST
HARD NUT RATING: 8.3
HARDOMETER
CUNNING: 9
COURAGE: 9
SURVIVAL SKILLS: 6
RUTHLESSNESS: 9

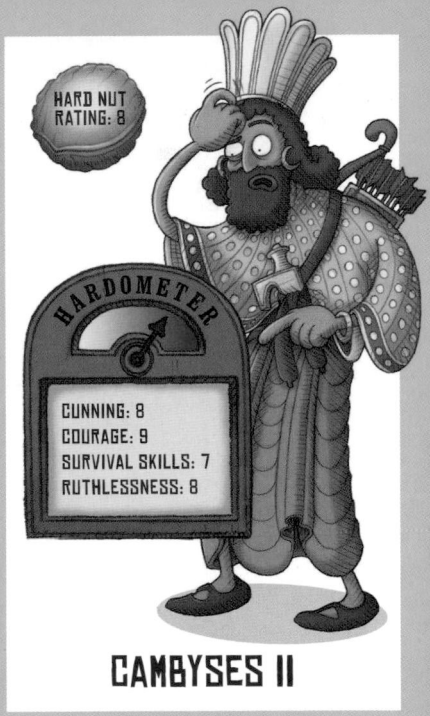
HARD NUT RATING: 8
HARDOMETER
CUNNING: 8
COURAGE: 9
SURVIVAL SKILLS: 7
RUTHLESSNESS: 8
CAMBYSES II

HARD NUT RATING: 5
HARDOMETER
CUNNING: 6
COURAGE: 7
SURVIVAL SKILLS: 5
RUTHLESSNESS: 2
QUETZALCOATL

BURKE AND WILLS
HARDOMETER
CUNNING: 5
COURAGE: 8
SURVIVAL SKILLS: 4
RUTHLESSNESS: 8
HARD NUT RATING: 6.3

HARD NUTS OF HISTORY

A & C BLACK
AN IMPRINT OF BLOOMSBURY
LONDON NEW DELHI NEW YORK SYDNEY

HARD NUTS OF HISTORY

A & C BLACK
AN IMPRINT OF BLOOMSBURY
LONDON NEW DELHI NEW YORK SYDNEY

HARD NUTS OF HISTORY

A & C BLACK
AN IMPRINT OF BLOOMSBURY
LONDON NEW DELHI NEW YORK SYDNEY

HARD NUTS OF HISTORY

A & C BLACK
AN IMPRINT OF BLOOMSBURY
LONDON NEW DELHI NEW YORK SYDNEY

ATHENS
ALCIBIADES
HARD NUT RATING: 7.8
SPARTA
HARDOMETER
CUNNING: 9
COURAGE: 5
SURVIVAL SKILLS: 8
RUTHLESSNESS: 9

CARACTACUS
HARD NUT RATING: 8.8
HARDOMETER
CUNNING: 8
COURAGE: 9
SURVIVAL SKILLS: 10
RUTHLESSNESS: 8

AHMOSE I
HARD NUT RATING: 8.8
HARDOMETER
CUNNING: 8
COURAGE: 9
SURVIVAL SKILLS: 9
RUTHLESSNESS: 9

BOUDICA
HARD NUT RATING: 7.5
HARDOMETER
CUNNING: 7
COURAGE: 9
SURVIVAL SKILLS: 7
RUTHLESSNESS: 7

HARD NUTS OF HISTORY

A & C BLACK
AN IMPRINT OF BLOOMSBURY
LONDON NEW DELHI NEW YORK SYDNEY

HARD NUTS OF HISTORY

A & C BLACK
AN IMPRINT OF BLOOMSBURY
LONDON NEW DELHI NEW YORK SYDNEY

HARD NUTS OF HISTORY

A & C BLACK
AN IMPRINT OF BLOOMSBURY
LONDON NEW DELHI NEW YORK SYDNEY

HARD NUTS OF HISTORY

A & C BLACK
AN IMPRINT OF BLOOMSBURY
LONDON NEW DELHI NEW YORK SYDNEY

DAVID LIVINGSTONE
HARD NUT RATING: 7.5
HARDOMETER
CUNNING: 6
COURAGE: 10
SURVIVAL SKILLS: 9
RUTHLESSNESS: 5

FUMO LIYONGO
HARD NUT RATING: 6.5
HARDOMETER
CUNNING: 9
COURAGE: 7
SURVIVAL SKILLS: 5
RUTHLESSNESS: 5

HARD NUT RATING: 8
HARDOMETER
CUNNING: 8
COURAGE: 6
SURVIVAL SKILLS: 8
RUTHLESSNESS: 10
ASHURNASIRPAL II

SIEGFRIED SASSOON
HARD NUT RATING: 7.5
HARDOMETER
CUNNING: 7
COURAGE: 9
SURVIVAL SKILLS: 7
RUTHLESSNESS: 7

HARD NUTS OF HISTORY

A & C BLACK
AN IMPRINT OF BLOOMSBURY
LONDON NEW DELHI NEW YORK SYDNEY

HARD NUTS OF HISTORY

A & C BLACK
AN IMPRINT OF BLOOMSBURY
LONDON NEW DELHI NEW YORK SYDNEY

HARD NUTS OF HISTORY

A & C BLACK
AN IMPRINT OF BLOOMSBURY
LONDON NEW DELHI NEW YORK SYDNEY

HARD NUTS OF HISTORY

A & C BLACK
AN IMPRINT OF BLOOMSBURY
LONDON NEW DELHI NEW YORK SYDNEY